WORDS
BEFORE DAWN

POEMS

WORDS
BEFORE DAWN

WILLIAM WENTHE

LOUISIANA STATE UNIVERSITY PRESS
BATON ROUGE

Published by Louisiana State University Press
Manufactured in the United States of America
LSU Press Paperback Original

Designer: Barbara Neely Bourgoyne
Typeface: Whitman

Library of Congress Cataloging-in-Publication Data
Wenthe, William, 1957–
  Words before dawn : poems / William Wenthe.
      p. cm.
  "LSU Press Paperback Original."
  ISBN 978-0-8071-4481-7 (pbk. : alk. paper) — ISBN 978-0-8071-4482-4 (pdf) — ISBN 978-0-8071-4483-1
(epub) — ISBN 978-0-8071-4484-8 (mobi)
  I. Title.
  PS3573.E565W67 2012
  811'.54—dc23

                                                                                    2011050508

The author would like to thank the editors of the following journals, in which the poems listed first appeared:
AGNI online: "Goldsmith and Charity" and "What They Made from Its Bones"; *Ascent:* "North Creek";
Callaloo: "Reading" and "The Literalist"; *Cave Wall:* "The Worker at Babel"; *Georgia Review:* "November:
Journal Entry"; *Greensboro Review:* "Parked beneath a Pear Tree"; *Harvard Review:* "In the Studio, 1949";
Image: "Stone on Stone: Israel, 1980"; *ISLE:* "In a Coastal B&B"; *Margie:* "Poem before Breakfast"; *Ninth
Letter:* "Great-Tailed Grackle"; *Northwest Review:* "Pink Sheet"; *Ontario Review:* "Budapest"; *Paris Review:*
"Picture of the Author with Vice President"; *Passages North:* "The House of Fabergé"; *Poetry:* "Poorwill"; *Poetry
East:* "The Job"; *Sewanee Review:* "Infant Father"; *Southern Review:* "Ballooning," "'Omit Needless Words,'"
"*Uhte*," "Universes," and "Winter Dusk"; *Southwest Review:* "Emmaus" and "Platonic"; *Sou'wester:* "From Far
Away"; *Stand Magazine* (U.K.): "Bird Market on the Île de la Cité"; *Tin House:* "From the Travel Journals of
Bashō: August 1684"; *Western Humanities Review:* "Foundation Myth" and "Music and Suicide."

"Infant Father" and "Picture of the Author with Vice President" were featured on *Poetry Daily* (www.poems
.com); "Platonic" was featured on *Verse Daily* (www.versedaily.com); "Poorwill" was reprinted in *The Poets'
Guide to the Birds* (Anhinga Press, 2009).

The author is grateful for the Everett Southwest Literary Award, and to Texas Tech University, for significant
support in completing this collection.

He is also grateful for the kindness, inspiration, and attention of Bruce Beasley, Robert Cording, Loren
Graham, Jacqueline Kolosov, Jeffrey Harrison, and Daniel Tobin, thanks to whom this book bears fewer flaws.
Thanks as well to Kelly Cherry, who read the manuscript for LSU Press and offered useful advice.

To Sophia and Jacqueline,
beckon and origin, both

As we are mock'd with art

—SHAKESPEARE

the happy eachness of all things

—W. H. AUDEN

CONTENTS

WORDS
BEFORE DAWN

POEM BEFORE BREAKFAST

O taste and see
—PSALM 34

All around me the little mouths
waiting to be fed. The two cats,
whimpering, ply their persuasions
among table legs; while outside
the starving window, a sparrow
chirps on the feeder's empty lip.
Back in my office, little boxes
on a form open their mouths
in triplicate, hungry
as the green lines of this page
I'm feeding with black spider-silk
of these lines, imagining
even the ghosts of this house,
whose bible and polaroids
we found in the attic,
linger, too, for a word.
Inside the deep belly
of that bible, each psalm
is a mouth for a hungry tribe
trying to feed itself
on a song, while here
on this broadcast plain,
the dawn opens red
against horizon-teeth of houses;
sunlight gnaws down from tops of oaks
to swallow us all again.

UHTE

Lately I've been waking with my infant daughter
in the hour before dawn.
We sit in the rocking chair as shades
outside the window begin their slow, emergent
separation: the darker mass of trees
looming against withdrawing, slate-toned sky
and a few stars, slightly smaller now, farther.

And I'm recalling, from my years' ago
study of Old English, a word, *uhte:*
"the hour before dawn." I've lost most
of that old tongue, but that word
has haunted me—wondering how that hour
had first called forth a need
to be distinguished by a sound.

Did that first, faint ash of light
augur grief, or gratefulness: *uht*-care
of the lamenting wife, or *uht*-song
of the monk's orison? For me,
in this fulcrum hour, it's a balance
between body's sleep-longing, and rest-
lessness of mind. But not for my daughter, full

awake, and writhing in my arms until
I have to set her down to crawl.
She keeps a running commentary as she goes,
in infant babble and chortle—but within it
a recurring sound, two syllables: distinctly
a word of her own making, whose meaning,
in her predawn of language, I can only try

to guess. Though hearing her, I'm just now
coming to realize how she's given

body to that ancient word
for an hour that most of my life
I've missed out on, but now share with her,
before it blurs into the light
of merely numbered hours.

READING

What crumbled from the book
like flakes of old paper
was a moth, somehow caught
between dustjacket and cover.

There it got crushed
against letters of the word
"Beauty" impressed in the spine,
so that the word BEAU
was outlined in silver
mothwing dust
against the dustjacket.

The moth died into a word.
The word was beautiful (in French).
Utterly literal, this death;
this *beau,* merely chance.
But caught up in being
human, how can I help
but read it that way?

THE HOUSE OF FABERGÉ

—A Natural History

MALLARD

For every living swatch
Of the bird's feathered livery,
A chosen stone matched:

An array of chalcedony
In gray, and jasper, and mottled
Brown to render belly,

Breast, and mantle;
White for the ring on its neck,
White and onyx for tail,

And mustard for the beak.
More precious stones—
Lapis lazuli, and opaque

Nephrite, from Siberian mines—
Give the speculum and head
Their Imperial sheen.

Seamlessly inlaid,
Each stone's incised
Like feathers; webbed gold

For feet, diamonds for eyes.
By virtue of this labor
Meant to disguise

Labor, he stands, a miniature
Marvel of recreated
Nature, no larger

Than a lady's wrist—aristocrat
Who sets it among bric-a-brac
In a glass cabinet.

Quel beau canard, she will cluck
To the visitor, in cultivated
French. *Canard*—a duck;

Or, in the less delicate
English tongue, a story hatched
To deceive, in a fashion most elaborate.

RAW MATERIAL

—Onot River, eastern Siberia

We have known the stones forever:
gray green on the gravel banks, or dark green
on river bottom, when water is summer low
and clear as the song of a wren.
The stones come smoothed and fit for the hand,
for a winter's lamplight carving.

Were men intended, as the emperor's men demand,
to dig these stones as boulders,
would the mountains grip so hard,
seal them in ice, cover themselves
in snow that takes a man's
feet from beneath him?

The dug rocks refuse to
balance. Tilted
with the pike, one boot-slip
and the boulder rolls back: the ankle bone
snaps like kindling, the eyes roll back,
white pebbles in the skull.
And so we're put to work. The oxen
shit with fright when the tackle drops
a boulder in the cart;
they rumble off, under the whip,
to God knows where. But a man

does not question the emperor's men.
Look, here, at my hands—
count my fingers, then count yours.
That is all I dare to say.

FABERGÉ, TO HIMSELF

En vain j'interoge . . . la nature et le Créateur
—GOUNOD, *Faust*

That a thing should be so perfectly itself—
beautiful *and* natural. I think of the ladies
outside the shop window, looking not *in*
at the jewelry, but *down* at something else.
I set aside the ledger, stepped outside to see:
it was a sparrow, flown into its own reflection
in the window glass, dazed on the sill.
A shabby, drab, brownish thing at first—
but the details: such patterning of rhodonite,
onyx, alabaster; such a layering of design.
I watch these ducks dabbling in the muck—
why should the mallard drake be so adorned?
We are customed to link such luxury
with ranks of nobility: so it is we see
in the generations of the czar, born to the regalia,
a command of beauty, symbolized each spring
by Imperial eggs that take a year to craft.

Yet all this finery, weighed against a feather
of the mallard's belly, shimmering with lines
of the finest *guilloche*, fails to compare.
What onyx, what black pearl, can render
the rounded luster of a mouse's eye?
What tiger-eye approximate—the tiger's eye?
So we take liberties, we miniaturize,
as if wonder grows as the creature
shrinks, to the measure of a finger,
a fingernail. Impossible that I should live
in the country, where the mushroom after rain,
and the casual river-stone, outdo me.
In my apartment, in a silver cage,
I keep a starling I have taught to whistle

a melody from Gounod's *Faust*.
It is a kind of bargain I have struck:
let the starlings try on our songs,
and I will spin gold into sprays of oats,
set diamonds for the eyes of mice.

ADVENT

December evening, frost embossed in curves
à l'art nouveau on windows, glossy black
inside the workshop, where Christmas orders from
the London branch have kept them at the bench.

Now, as if a wagon had bumped and burst
a crate of chickens on the cobbles, they step
slowly into the street, seen for the first
time in days. Dazed and dazzled, they huddle and gape
at windows candled gold, their trapezoids
of yellow light thrown down on sidewalk snow.
Compulsive clinking of the chasing hammers,
still ringing in their minds, subsides to sleighbells,
sigh of the runners, and horses' muffled hooves.

Champagne! The evening calls for it—but their throats
insist on vodka's quicker work. Yet, for now,
the evening is enough. Their eyes, long locked
to the jeweler's vise, the hammered shape, relax:
content to watch these others run their courses—
the veering sleighs, the rippling flanks of horses,
a servant opening an iron gate
to let a load of firewood come in;
and snowflakes, chatoyant, that falling, yaw
under lamplight, each in its eccentric way—
crystals chipped from the unseen face
of cloud, to touch a moment the open space
between hat and scarf with small, chill notes
like the bell-chime of a clock, and melt.
If one could stop the moment, sculpt them there,
the melting flakes might look like tears.

On Easter, 1885, Tsar Alexander III presented to his wife, the Empress
Maria, an egg crafted by the Fabergé studio. After his death, his son, Tsar
Nicholas III, continued this tradition, presenting Fabergé eggs to his wife,
the Empress Alexandra, and to the dowager Empress Maria.

The first egg was a golden egg, white enameled.
   Twist it and it opened to a golden yolk,
      Which opened to reveal a golden hen.
A jeweler's answer to the famous riddle?
   No, another question—a hatch in her back:
      Inside, a tiny, diamond, Imperial crown.

(Gaping, they must have wondered—*Where in hell*
   Does it come from, such wealth?—while they sacked
      Gatchina Palace.) The last egg was fashioned
In blackened steel, held up by small artillery shells.
      Then, revolution.

CANARD

In 1922 (Fabergé, having fled
the revolution, lies dead),
the Bolsheviks have banned
abstraction, demand
that art be representative.

What to make, then, of this *objet
de fantaisie*? A salt-cellar, crafted
in the form of a bidet—
a functional vessel
designed to represent
a vessel for bodily function.

Sepia and opalescent
enamel over turned gold
simulate the seat-back of brocade,
with seed-pearls for tacks;
its gold legs and frame
support a bowl of Siberian jade.

And where, in the real one, the urine
would go, now goes the pure,
Suprematist white of the salt
to savor the *haute cuisine*
of the epicure's table. Can we be sure
what's represented here? Is it a rich

joke upon the rich,
or fantastical object
to which workers should object?
"Save us from the abstract,"
declares the Soviet. And the jeweler:
"Deliver us from fact."

BIRD MARKET ON THE ÎLE DE LA CITÉ

Crowded in wire cages, some still sing.
I hear them from the stalls where merchants
provide us with loveliness, prisoned little things:

canaries and finches (prize cousins of the farthing
sparrow); cockatiels, parakeets, lovebirds, pigeons
crowded in wire cages. Some still sing.

Plumed crowns and crests, collars, bands, and rings;
turquoise, coral, saffron; feathered iridescence
to provide us with loveliness: prisoned little things

that do no work, and yet are robed like kings.
Seeds and sawdust, though, their meek inheritance,
crowded in wire cages. Some still sing—

if not the migrant blackbirds' rooftop songs,
or fulsome wren's, hidden in Luxembourg Gardens.
To provide us with loveliness, we prison little things

in a Sunday market, near the stone-carved wings
of the cathedral, where, away from apartments,
we crowd wire cages where some still sing:
provide us with loveliness, prisoned little things.

WHAT THEY MADE FROM ITS BONES

Buttons, of course. Dagger handles. Letter openers.
Hairpins, combs. Blemish powders to cover moles.
Clasps, stays, grommets, bobbins, brooches, splints.
Rattles, plectrums, rosary beads, and at least one
reliquary for a splinter of the cross. Cribbage
pegs, concertina keys, teething rings, teeth.
Sealing wax. Fertilizer for cabbages. Kings,
queens, bishops, knights, rooks, pawns. Whipstocks,
aphrodisiacs, laxatives. Pipe stems, crossbow ticklers . . .
An extinction so thorough, we find no remains
of the bird itself; only relics of a vanished
settlement, preserved for us in glass museum cases.

FOUNDATION MYTH

—New York, 1981

The exhausted reach
of an abandoned Westside pier
sagged under the weight
of its own gray timbers
and the sullen, two-way
tidal pull of the river.

And there, an improvised
dump: bottles, newsprint,
catalogs, rags, and, emerging
from the pile, neatly typed
sheets of paper. I picked one up:
a page from someone's novel.

In it, a man was speaking
to someone, and though it was only
small talk, I could feel,
underneath it, the pressure
to say something important;
but his words were cut off

by the end of the page.
Unable to finish the sentence,
I had to cringe
at the irony of it—so
contrived, it seemed, even if
true: for I had come to the dump

looking for some material
solid enough to support
a hollow-core, unhinged
door for a writing desk.
And I found it: old cobblestones,
black-flecked, sparkling—but

so heavy, I'd have to return,
again and again, to the dump.
With each haul, the irony wore
away, revealing, beneath it,
another: so much weight,
just to hold up words.

MUSIC AND SUICIDE

> To die at the Opéra by ingesting a hallucinatory opiate while listening
> to glorious music was the ideal of sentimental Romantics.
> —WILLIAM G. ATWOOD, *The Parisian Worlds of Frederick Chopin*

The surfeit of signage in cities
is stranger still in this city where "stranger"
is cognate with foreigner, which is what I am,
waking up over café in a café. Again,
scrambling up the Metro stairs, I found
myself suddenly in the middle of
a crowd in the middle of things, where attempts
at description bleed into macaronic
babble, a moribund abstraction, deadpan
as pedestrian faces. It's no wonder

the poems I find celebrated of late
by younger poets in cities have little
to say but sound, a nonchalance of nuance
where words become sound, and blur to surd.
Music, I suppose, is at least a mode
of order, a way of connecting, counter
to the bird-banishing height of buildings,
the gray noise of sandblasters on scaffolds,
and the mass isolation of traffic where self
seems no more than a word, and a word a cipher,
meaningless, by itself, as a semiquaver.

Or so they've been taught by their teachers:
that the old Whitmanic "I," who assumed
responsibility for what he names, ferrying outward
and back, in the horsemeat brawl of his Manhattan,
has been fragmented, webbed, or murdered.
Or, is it suicide? In Paris, in the 1840s,
a society was founded, its members devoted
to suicide. An exclusive, artistic club—no one

over thirty, and only those refined enough
to savor the tragic loneliness of
an artist in the city. They'd theorize the means
of crafting that supreme rejection—self-
annihilation—but leaving no blemish
on the body, for the gesture's beauty required
an exquisite corpse, in frock-coat and polished
boots, perhaps, succumbed to opium
in delirious arias at the opera. It was all
conceptual. Only one member resigned
the club by actually doing himself in.
Meanwhile, for those dullard citizens
suffering their uninspired but unbearable pain,
there hung a net of chains across the Seine
to catch their bloated, fish-pocked bodies.

Music and suicide. They're in vogue, again.
Here in this café, I try to piece myself
together, among screaming signs and silent
faces, panoplies of fashions and pigeons strutting
into my attention and gone. In this middle
of this middle, I think I can grasp
that longing for an ending, that final
note. All these young Werthers, but cagier—
they get the joke. He killed himself
at his writing desk. Me, I'd rather risk living.

IN THE STUDIO: 1949

Django Reinhardt is unsatisfied
with the rhythm section, so he plays
louder, till it's mostly himself
backing up Stéphane Grappelli on "La Mer,"
whose violin's relishing that melody, all
arabesque and sweetness, lofty and light
and swirled as meringue. And when it's time
for Django to take the lead, and he hits
that first high A, his finger (one of two
on his left hand not deformed
and paralyzed when the candle kissed
the celluloid flowers, and the whole
caravan swelled with flames) holds
a perfect note—such attack and sustain,
haloed with overtones, trembling
with faint vibrato: as though he'd been born
for no purpose other than that hand—
the hand he'd fought the doctors not
to amputate—should find that note.
Two measures later, the melody calls
for that note again, but it's not there:
instead, a weak glissando, mumbled
slur across the frets; then slurred again—
is it that musician's trick, to repeat
the error, make it seem intended?
Or is it a refusal? As though,
by denying the condition of music,
he could tolerate the condition of
history. In Paris, during the war,
musicians beat the time
of curfew by staying inside
the clubs, and jamming till dawn.
To fool the Nazis, they disguised
the banned word *blues* as the French *tristesse*,
a sadness. Sometimes

a regular customer, hardly noticed
until the night that he's not there:
not there, and never there again.
And from time to time, stories—
of gypsies in prison camps who claimed
to be Django, hoping it might save them;
later, of foreign papers reporting, from time
to time, his death.

            Now, that haunting note
behind him, Django aspires to the lowest
notes on the neck, plays them surly
and sullen; against the beat, staccato
strikes against the melody: hammers, digs
his way down, through. Improvise. Solo.

FROM THE TRAVEL JOURNALS OF BASHŌ: AUGUST 1684

After his mother has died, and after his small house has burned to the ground, Bashō journeys forth, to seek the permanent good he calls "poetry." He travels by foot, through days of steady rain. One morning, along the Fuji River, he comes upon a boy, about three years old, alone and crying on the shore. It seems he has been abandoned there. His parents, Bashō can only surmise, had thought the boy unsuitable for this life, this life which—and at this point, he gazes toward the rain-swollen river—

> *flows as turbulent*
> *as fanged and coiled currents,*
> *the Fuji in flood.*

By contrast, it seems this child will live no longer than . . . than what? He turns to the sodden meadow. —*Than the morning dew, that glistens on grass.* As Bashō studies the boy, sobbing, coughing on mucus and tears, he sees, for a moment, a purity of suffering, in

> *a child so fragile—*
> *petals dropping at merest*
> *breath of autumn wind.*

From his satchel he removes pen and paper, along with the little bit of food he carries, a portion fit for an old monk, or for one, like Bashō, seeking a monk's disposition. The boy does not eat. Bashō thinks of the ancient poet who was moved to tears at the sad cries of monkeys. What would *he* have thought of this child? So Bashō now composes a haiku on that theme, in a slight, but acceptable, variation of the form. And following the way that one question will lead to a further question, Bashō asks: What is the cause of such misery? The boy still wails, as Bashō raises his eyes to the gray inkwash of sky.

> *It is to heaven,*
> *raining in autumn, you must*
> *direct your lament.*

Then Bashō moves on, leaving the child to die.

PICTURE OF THE AUTHOR WITH VICE PRESIDENT

2001–2008

That's me on his left. If neither one of us
looks comfortable, it's because I said
I'm sorry to hear about his heart.
A small machine, he says, sends tiny sparks
in there, to pace the flow of blood.
Some people will dispute this photo; his office
has denied it's me; but I have to believe
I *am* in the picture. It's awkward, yes,
for we don't know each other;
and if he's known as a man who keeps
public secrets, I'm not known at all.
Even so, he and I share something
that we cherish, deeply, which is our love

of trout. On his western ranch, he owns
a trout stream for himself. When I raise
the question—How's the fishing?—he will rise
to the subject, and we will have grown
a little closer, having now disclosed
a passion no one, having known, lets go.
And he, too, is a man who knows cold blood
of trout cares nothing for who you are.
Nor do they care who owns the land
their water flows within: so long
as land and stream stay clean, they live.
Because I must rely on public lands
to find—weighed out in the flash
of a trout's brilliant scales—that cleanly order,
I'm concerned about his sympathy
with those who call such places "undeveloped."
But I know better than to say as much
to a man who's so well versed
in the rhyming of "ecology" with "economy"—

abstract nets that hold so many tangibles,
such as meadow grass that filters silt
so cutthroat trout may have clean beds
of gravel for their spawning redds;
or the English teacher whose hopes
for a pay raise float on the promise
of a growing tax base—in other words,
the new sportcoat I'm wearing
in the photo, bought for this occasion.
Still, I want to believe in the heart
of a man who would fish a barbless fly
for a trout, and let it go; who would spend
that much time to be where trout live, to step
so softly in their stream, they do not frighten.

So I am going to tell him a story
about the Sacramento Mountains of New Mexico,
and a man who lived there. By all accounts,
William Myers knew the land, but owned
none of it. Had no money, so in order to live
in the mountains, he bartered work
for the privilege of staying in
other people's second homes.
One day, he drove his ATV up a ridge
to scout the most likely route to run a pipe
to his friend's house. He lit a cigarette,
studied the forest floor, as he'd often done
for fresh deer lies, bear scat, a crop of mast
that might draw wild turkeys in.
Whether it was a spark from the ATV
or the cigarette, he didn't know; but he was sure,
he told police, that it was he who caused the fire.
That night, a glowing orange blemish on the sky;
by next day a dry mist with a taste
of wet paper. Nine thousand acres
of forest he had hunted, ponds and creeks
he'd fished—the bell-note of hummingbird wings,

the raccoon crooning to her pups—gone up
in a surf of flame; sap-laden pines burst
like the improvised gas-and-bottle bombs
he'd learned to make in the army. Helicopters
dropped fire-retardant chemicals on a woods
he'd loved but never owned, and never meant

to burn. They fell in scarlet plumes, like blood
that must have sprayed from his skull
when he stood in front of the gun
he held in his own hand, and fired.
—Well, it may have been the words
like blood, and skull, and gun,
that made the men in sunglasses bring
our conversation to a polite, efficient end.
Or it could have been my agitation
over a man who took responsibility—
who, as his scribbled farewell letter read,
could never live with what he had destroyed.

IN A COASTAL B&B

It makes no difference, she writes,
where I sit when I write: enough
for me in this back kitchen—
formica table, toaster chrome,

a window without counterweights
I've propped open with a pot.
The green gazebo and the rosy porch
are lovely, lovelier now they're weaned

from the industrialist who raised them
on the sooty lungs of workers.
But the porch is for hollyhocks,
and the clop-clop of horse-drawn

nostalgia; for thickest creams to swirl
in coffee, its beans fetched far
as jungles of dangling lianas
where this toucan sitting on a milking stool

had yawped once, were it real. This B&B's
another place to come and feel
out of place, to fabricate
from literal grit of A, B, C's,

another place to come and feel. *My jungles
verge on coffee fields*, the toucan might have said,
were his beak of cyan, yellow, red,
not sewn shut with polyester thread. . . .

Outside, the fraternizing *yuk* of gulls,
the conversations on the porch. But she
stays here and writes, and takes another cup
of coffee, drinking jungles sip by sip.

BUDAPEST

I

Chapel bell in walnut roots,
Chestnut leaves and boles.
Two hawks: one bronze
And mythical, one feathered
And flying over verdigris
Palace roof. Minor scales
On hammered strings
Of cimbalom; granite stairs,
Fishface spigot speaking
Water tongues, and nine-star crown,
Stained-glass sunshafts on
Rose-petal pilasters. Fan-
Leafed plane tree spans a wing
Over Beethoven tympanum,
Frogs, a squeaking bat.
O robed girl, stuck
In a stucco cornice—
Feet on one side, face on the other . . .
Or are you flying through?

II

Starved centaur,
Foreleg bandaged,
Crutch beneath the human
Arm. Bronze fixations:
Warmen, liberators, pocked
By acid weather, arm in sling,
A robed and plinthed
Anonymous. Stench
Of spraycan fumes, bench-
Bound boy, babbling, sticky

Sock in sniffing hand.
Gray stone sooted grayer,
Soviet bas-relief, deadpan
Workers, hands more mass
Than heads. Pigeons older
Than Stalin and Hitler.
Pastel stucco crumble.
In each red velvet opera
Booth, a gilt-framed mirror.

III

One afternoon, crossing the Chain Bridge from Buda to Pest,
(for this city is two cities), I noticed,
chained to the railing between sidewalk and traffic lane,
a small bucket planted, it seemed, with a tree.
I say a tree—it was a mere trunk, about five feet high,
limbs lopped right to the base.
One notices such things and forgets them. . . .
Or notices, the next day, that it's not there. . . .
Or dismisses it as a pickpocket's decoy,
or bait to get some sort of swindle going,
like the yellow knapsack that lay like a golden egg on Vaci Street. . . .
It was days before I noticed a similar tree
on the corner below the hotel—but sculpted in bronze,
set in a concrete niche, protected by an iron grille.

A plaque above it, though printed in brass,
said as little to me as the spraycan insignias of graffiti
that braid the foundations of buildings throughout the city—
whether Gothic, Ottoman, Hapsburg, Soviet, corporate—
Nor did I mind, for this unreadability
seemed accurate enough, for the uncountable ways,
the thousand thousand thousand turns, splendid and squalid,
whereby a city—baroque interiors, bronzed public postures—
comes into being:

before an advancing army, the monks are hiding
the sacred treasures of their order. Centuries later, in a great storm,
a walnut tree overturns, reveals
among its roots a chapel bell.

STONE ON STONE: ISRAEL, 1980

I stood in the Jaffa Gate and played harmonica for tips. A cluster of men in Arab dress surrounded me, bewildered, smiling. They had never heard a harmonica before, nor could they see, behind my hands, this sound I held to my lips.

The long cry of the *muezzin*, undulating among corbelled roofs, towers, calling the souls to prayer.

Never coffee so bitter, halvah so sweet. And two kinds of currency: pounds and sheqels. The old and the new. Or, the old and the older.

I intended to buy a wedding present for friends back home. A carpet, I thought, as I wandered the stone streets, stone alleyways, stone-covered galleries. Dead ends. Corners; shadows . . . Black portals, cats. I kept arriving at the sign: *Street of Chains.*

Throughout the New City, sirens wailed. Everyone stopped. Crowds of shoppers stopped. Pedestrians crossing the street stopped in the traffic lanes. Traffic stopped. Persons on stairs stood still, one foot lifted to the next step. A man holding a door open held the door open; the old woman in the doorway stopped. For the duration of sirens, no one moved, no one spoke. An orange dropped from a shopper's bag, rolled down the curb. . . .

In a turn of a stone stairway, in its dry half-light, a man offered to buy my blood. He accosted me there, told me his brother is in the hospital, in dire need of blood. Of course it was insane; of course the intention, whatever it could be, was criminal. Yet I could not get away from him—had to stand there, find a way to explain why I would not give, or even sell, my blood to him.

Two Bedouin women, seated on paving stones old as Herod, only their eyes and hands appearing from robes and veils. For sale on a blanket before them, cheeses wrapped in palm leaves. White as bone, dry as sand, tasting mainly of salt.

Sirocco—sandy grit in the teeth. A sunbird hovering by the tumbling springs of Ein Gedi. And in the desert, by the border with Jordan, the Indian silverbill nests in the razor wire.

The men could only hear the sounds escaping from behind my hands, thin reeds echoing in stones of the vaulted gate.

I asked someone, what just happened? He said the sirens are to remember the Holocaust.

Inside the shrine, a man of indeterminate age polishes marble. Rapid and constant he's swirling the soft brown cloth. On his knees, bent like a supplicant, polishing, polishing. Eyes fixed on the marble floor—no, on something further—polishing.

A parade passed before us in celebration of Israeli independence. She said she could not wait to begin her military service. She was seventeen, an antelope, her eyes like doves'.

In the Moslem quarter, I bought a slice of halvah, handing the merchant a ten-pound note for one pound's worth of halvah. The merchant refused to give me change until I could tell him when the conflict had begun. 1967, I said. He said come back when you know. I came back the next day—1948. No, he said, come back when you know. I dug around in a book, and returned the next day. About 1200 BC the Israelites conquered Palestine.

See? He said. We were here first!
Then he gave me my change, as if I had earned it.

As if everything, no matter how routine, must be taken by a form of struggle. The everyday work of it, the sheer prose of it, the Street of Chains of it. The first time I heard the question, as the uniformed guard pointed to my bag: Did you pack this yourself? The most ordinary gesture attended by generations of enmity; the only assumption—a condition of war, for what looked like, as I rode the taxi from the airport, a land of rocks. Who was I, but a kid from the leafy suburbs? But I knew that. And that was why I had come.

Here is the place where Christ died. And here is the other place where Christ died.

At any moment, unplanned, the sirens. All that noise, and the weight of silence.

I went to the site of the pool where Christ healed the sick. Peering down the rectangular stonewalled pit at the mossy water far below, I could not configure how people had managed to bathe in it. Clearly some dramatic change had occurred over the centuries. Then a dazzling flash of electric blue—a kingfisher —flew up from the water.

I played harmonica till my lips were sore. Scottish airs, blues, a little Gershwin. Only tourists gave me any tips. Could it be they thought I was part of the city, what they had come to see?

Noting the camera around my neck, an old man brandished his cane. He'll strike if I shoot.

I found a merchant whose rugs I admired, but they were all too expensive. Come with me, he said, I have more in my house. I followed him through narrow stone lanes, up a stone stairway. We entered his house; I nodded to his family, and he led me to a larger room, layered with carpets. He showed me the rug I wanted, but still too expensive. I am a poor person, I said; I saved for a year to visit this land; I have spent almost all my money; I am leaving in two days. He said I am offering you a deal; my profit is very low to begin with; I am making no money on this. And he turned to praising the quality of the rug—the wool, the dyes, the loomwork. I praised its virtue as a wedding gift, extolled the motive of love—that this piece will warm the sparse apartment of newlyweds was a kind of value beyond money. But: I am driving a poor merchant into bankruptcy, stealing food from the mouths of his children, depriving his wife of clothes, denying his mother a decent funeral. But: he is robbing me, he is cheating a man far away from home, a traveller, a wandering guest here; he is insulting my friend, he is stealing the food I would eat tomorrow. After half an hour we agreed on a price: ninety sheqels. We exchanged money and carpet; we fought to see who could thank each other the more profusely.

The next day I saw the same carpet on the wall of a different shop, the list price: ninety sheqels. I considered what a bargain I'd made: for the same price, not only the carpet but the food from his children's mouths, his wife's clothing, and an old woman's funeral.

Nobody told me about the airport tax. Even if you already have your ticket in hand, you have to lay out cash in order to leave. I had wired to send the rest of my savings to Athens—a lot of good that does me here. I have no money. I have twenty-four hours. I have a tiny instrument with bendable reeds.

WINTER DUSK

—New York, 1981

Snow in the act of falling,
   silent and undriven,
seems selflessly unwilling
   to refuse what shapes are given
to veil in its unveiling.

No step of fire escape,
   no iron ladder rung,
no windowsill, no drainpipe lip,
   no granite cherub's wing
or paper coffee cup

too exalted or bereft
   to receive the evening snow
and mold the mounting drift
   whereby the shapes below
give shape to what they lift.

This white allays all noise,
   in dusklight seems to glow
and ask me if I dare embrace
   this city like the snow
that doesn't have a choice.

EMMAUS

—after Rembrandt

"Ordinary": the standard menu of an inn.
The three travelers have ordered. For it is toward
evening: what's left of a day far spent
spreads across the table, as the sun goes under
the hills they had crossed. One traveler, the strange one
who all afternoon wavered in the attention
of the two companions (their eyes lowered, being held
to the road and some tomb-business in Jerusalem)—
this man now breaks the loaf of bread, and his body
dawns from the wall-shadow, and luminous,
looms before them in the full, and the mere,
presence of a person, a piece of bread in hand.

NORTH CREEK

Years since I've fished here.
But still familiar,
this oak-hickory woods,
dusky streambed stones,
and deep green laurels.
If only I could see my friend Loren,
who first brought me to this water.

I remember that he used to tie,
just for this stream, his own version
of the fly named the Royal Trude;
an "attractor" pattern, so called,
because it imitates nothing
a trout would feed upon naturally.

When Loren gets to tying them,
they look even less like the nothing
in nature the ideal pattern
represents, meant to mimic
only itself. Though we've both moved
a thousand miles from here
in different directions, still I carry
a few in my vest— homespun
originals, scruffy but earnest,
hard-worked and hilarious.

So thinking of Loren, I tie one on,
and offer it all afternoon
until the trout have toothed it down
to threadbare hook. With each strike,
I savor my friend's approach
to this water: how,
if it doesn't quite look like food,
then perhaps it might assume
the shape of hunger.

GROUCHO AND TOM

In June 1964, T. S. Eliot hosted dinner for Groucho
Marx at Eliot's London flat.

Tom, with a bitter twist
of lemon, puts a closure on the shaken
martinis. Groucho wants to know about
"These fragments I have shored against my ruin."
But Tom, primed with a sip of gin, recites
a gag from *Animal Crackers,* and waits.

"Did I say that?" says Groucho.
Weeks ago, he had resolved to make
a "Literary Evening" of it; studied
The Waste Land and *Murder in the Cathedral,*
tossing in *King Lear* as a backup
in case the conversation ran thin.
Eliot, meanwhile, had taken his young wife
to a revival of *The Marx Brothers Go West.*
No wonder, then, midway into a tender roast,
the talk comes down to an aged Lear's
"Is man no more than this"
contending with crosstalk and malaprops
of the trial scene in *Duck Soup. . . .*

It was three years earlier that Eliot wrote
to request an autographed photo,
which he set in his office, between Valéry
and Yeats. But no one recognized the comedian
"without the cigar and rolling eyes,"
as Eliot phrased the delicate point
to Groucho, who gladly sent another,
this time in character, with trademark
cigar, greasepaint brows and moustache.
Likewise, T. S.—"Just how *do* I address you?"
wrote Groucho—sent a favorite photo,

of a smartly dressed, younger man;
but thinking better of it, later sent
a portrait that revealed himself
closer to his present age.

What a brilliant and rollicking dinner—
had only J. Alfred Prufrock and Rufus T. Firefly
arrived. But now, the after-dinner cheese
removed, only two old men are here, to face
each other, across a table. Time
for the living room, to linger
over a vintage port. They talk
of weather, and cats, and good cigars. . . .
well into the pleasing night.

THE LITERALIST

On gospel television, he preaches science:
a desert prophet, who wears a white lab coat
like a surplice, carries a clipboard
the way that Moses holds the tablets.
What moves me most, and draws me back
to hear him talk, is how he strains
between the bodied life of earth, and his belief
that all the words come straight from God.
He's a man of science, wounded and crossed
by science, who believes the bible as one
must believe a *theory:* one part wrong,
and the whole thing's blown to hell.

As to dinosaurs, he accepts the fossil record,
but carefully explains how God
had Noah save these enormous beasts
by carrying them into the ark
—as babies! And as to why no stegosaurs
cavorting in my garden like the possum
who grins the same Cretaceous grin
he'd grinned at dinosaurs, the literalist says—
I heard him say it—extinction's all in God's
great plan: the death that Adam brought to earth
by eating of the Tree. To prove his point,
he fixed a transparency to a light box
such as doctors use for x-rays: painted images
of vanished creatures; and as he named the animals,
he stumbled on a certain bird, and at first
I felt embarrassment for him, then shame:
he couldn't even name the passenger pigeon.
My God—there once were billions of them:
their migrations made a weather of their own
as they passed over, darkening the sky.
Shot down by wagonloads, fed to hogs—
the last one died in a zoo.

Still, he is just one man. No industry
bankrolls him, in that one-camera studio
somewhere on the Southwest borderland.
(I've heard him speak entire shows in Spanish.)
Aggrieved, he implores us to listen
to reason—reason as recorded, he'll say, once
and forever, in the bible. Which is where I come
to a question: if scripture says—and it does—
that none but God created all the animals—
beast, fish, and fowl—and commanded Noah save
every bird of every sort, then how can I see
a robin tilt its head, querying the crawlings
in the lawn, or pass through the gates
of a shopping mall and see the pigeons
crapping, scrapping there, and not fall down,
quaking, to my knees, in homage to these,
the living leavings of a loving Lord?

THE WORKER AT BABEL

Ever since Cain built a city, and Enos
called upon the name of the Lord,
we've been mad for both. So we thought
we'd build our city up to heaven:
the elders spoke, and everybody heard.
It was splendid work—I was foreman on top.
We were years into it, and then a moment
when I called down for more bricks,
and I might as well have spilled a hod
on their heads, the way they squawked.
I barked back at them, and so it went,
bleatings and gabblings down the stories.
It was almost comical—not such a racket,
I suppose, since the ark thumped Ararat.
I found my kinsmen and my in-laws,
and we went forth and multiplied
the earth with new names. Lord,
it was Adam all over again. One of the names
was Babel—in another tongue it means
Gates of God. Because it was a way in:
though not, as we'd thought, through heaven.

THE JOB

For many years I was self-appointed inspector of snow storms
and rain storms.
　　　—THOREAU

After he retired, he took another job. It amazed him
how much work there was to do. . . . Sundogs
in the five o'clock sky, the inca dove
sidling down a branch to its mate,
the apron of moss under a faucet—
all these things needing attention. How a man,
smoking outside a service entrance,
turns, with each savored puff, a slightly different direction.

He's often partnered in his rounds
with a gray-muzzled spaniel, off the leash,
whose nose and random ways discover
things a human, differently endowed, will miss:
once it was a possum hiding in a storm drain,
once a dead waxwing, glistening ants in attendance.
Somebody must see to all this business
no spreadsheet has accounted for: squirrel's claws
on a tin roof, the ways of raindrops on pine needles.

Surely there are jobs more peculiar: there was a boy
who walked Bonito Creek each night, calling owls
for a conservation survey; or the Errol Flynn look-alike
whom Warner Brothers hired just to sit
quietly in the commissary at lunchtime,
reminding the scandalous icon that his face
was only a commodity, readily replaced.

But in this job, with unlimited openings
and no description, no one is expendable.
Nor any reports to file—for how to summarize
the unclassified unique? Today it was a wren

with a june bug in its beak, pruned roses under a bush
beside a pair of garden gloves—these envelopes
of notice that keep opening for him, in ever
unfolding, moment by moment, payday.

POORWILL

An eruption from under-hedge, fluttering and dodging
like a moth in a surfeit of light—
with everywhere to turn, turns everywhere—
as if buffeted by wind of its own
wings; then swoops close, hangs a moment
sun-pinioned, wings shot
with light, barred buff-tones and grays
like an x-ray, pinned
in my eyes; only to crumple, and leaf-sway across
courtyard to shadowed foyer,
perching on threshold, a dark knot; then upswerves
to a cornice, brief gargoyle,
and flushes, caroms, corners the building—and gone.

Goatsucker, nightjar: names given the family
of birds, nocturnal, exquisitely feathered to blend
into leafmold, treebark, gravelbed. This bird
I know enough not to recognize
so I search in a book, and find it—poorwill,
this flurry of simile, and a half-swallowed whimper,
wishing only to be invisible.

BALLOONING

They shimmered before crowds at the football game;
cars at traffic lights saw them float,
as if the glint had lifted off windshields,
risen in wisps of mere light.

They hung from trees, from telephone lines;
a pine in the park was said to resemble
a Christmas tree spun with tinsel.
"City Mystified," the local paper said.

And in Dallas, thousands called police,
suspicious of these waves of gossamer
crossing backyard fences, infiltrating lawns.
Meanwhile, on twig-tips, newly born

spiderets, pale-green asterisks, extrude
strands of silk which then suspend
in air; extending further until the air
lifts both strand and spider, as a man

might cling to the tether of an escaped
balloon—except there is no balloon,
only silk tethered to nothing, glossed
with sun. And this is called "ballooning."

And this, considered by the thousands:
a townscape hatched with glowing lines,
scrolls of flowing script inviting us
to look again at where we live.

To think, that fall, of all that fell,
yet this, too, had made the news:
baby spiders riding wind
to routine death, or luck of a twig.

UNIVERSES

Mountain Chickadee
A name at once so big, so small.

April Storm
Pear blossoms and snowfall, and not a metaphor.

My Daughter's Toes
Fresh from the amniotic sea, this pink anemone.

Hummingbird Nest (I)
She harvests cobwebs under the soffit.

Garden Prohibition
The Monarch is poison to the Kingbird.

Cave Swallow
What the cave does, or where the swallow lives?

Mockingbird
Pays no royalties on borrowed tunes.

Mantis
Praying or Preying, I can never remember.

Daughter at Six Months
I point to the clouds but she's looking at starlings.

Hummingbird Nest (II)
This plum-sized cup of lichen and web—how did I find it?

Stepping on an Ant
Not if it were my size.

Mosquito
When I slap her, it's my own blood she bleeds.

Nighthawk in Daylight
I'm not on the branch because I'm a knot on the branch.

Owl in Daylight
Swirl of orioles, shrieks of chickadees.

September Rains
On the playground, an avocet wades by the swingset.

October Garden
A starling struts in the cosmos.

Extinction
An elephant carved out of ivory.

Silence
Snowflakes whiten the windchimes, slowly.

After the Ice Storm: Pipit
Slips and falls on his little feathered ass.

Screech Owl
I'd call it tremolo-with-a-dying-fall owl.

Daughter at One Year
When I show her the pear blossoms, she points to the day moon.

"OMIT NEEDLESS WORDS"

But *is* there such a thing?
The first words ever uttered—
Let there be—required a universe
to answer them. The mother
names her child fifty ways; his
brothers name him fifty more:
such the range of need between
fraternal fondness and despite;
but that's to say nothing
of how a word needs other words:
when I say *Strunk,* how it begs
for *White;* how, say, the word *ring*
will insist upon *engagement,* and *wedding,*
or *benzene* or *boxing* or *bull.*
Even the smallest—the shorthand
ampersand, that hatchling in the nest—
how it cries for connection, the gaping
hunger of syntax, stuttering
&, &, & . . .

GREAT-TAILED GRACKLE

Quiscalus mexicanus

Had the Greeks such grackles,
    Socrates might have cackled
        a proof, to hear you squawk

your name. But speak again
    and rebuke him: such barbaric
        banging on a brazen pot,

such clatter as Cratylus
    could stuff down the wattled throat
        of the bickering Athenian.

Let them prattle of Truth. For who
    is more surprised than you
        by your own voice?

How you huff your shoulders
    like a bodybuilder, lower
        your head, crane your neck

till feathers prickle,
    and yellow eyes boggle
        at —*what-the-hell-was-that?*

—two whistles, lark-sweet,
    a radio static crackle
        and hiss, a bacon-fat

squeal and gurgle, punctuated
    by a sort of self-inflicted
        Heimlich Maneuver.

At home in the most
  unheimlich of places—
    airport and parking garage—

you drag that purple
    prow of tail feathers, magpie-
      proud, and promenading, stage

your courtship display, pointing
    skyward your beak,
      as if to gimlet

a hole in heaven
    until that telltale tail
      molts away in autumn,

leaves you strutting
    like a stunted, bobble-
      headed chicken;

but even then, you wear
    a minor goddess
      on your back—Iris

of iridescence—and you
    who stand for nothing
      else: you wallow in your noise.

PLATONIC

I hung a bedsheet on the study window,
    a screen to help me read the screen
of my computer, so awash with sun
    I couldn't see the cursor's arrow.

And while I'm at my desk, the driveway sparrows,
    crazy with mating season, flutter
back and forth from the telephone wire,
    and cast across the sheet their shadows

sharply drawn as Chinese shadow-theater,
    as ritualized, and as serious:
the males droop their wings, affect a pose,
    then give their wings a little shiver;

or squawk and squabble, sidestep down the line,
    fighting off the other males,
to where a female tenses, lifts her tail
    —to fly away, or let him in?

A shade set up for my computer screen
    becomes a screen where shadows play.
So is it love, or knowledge on display;
    which to study—shadow or gleam?

FROM FAR AWAY

> Is it love's trick of doubling?
> —WILLIAM MEREDITH

When I stepped outside this morning, frogs
   were making plaintive whistlings from the ditch
between the pasture and the railroad tracks.
   Stems of ditchbank brush inferred a touch
of gold. A quiver of red in the oaks.
   Evening now, and the frogs still whistle, each
to each—although from here they blend together
   so that I can't tell one voice from another.

The landscape offers up its casual
   allegories: the pull of a pair of bluebirds
tailing each other from grass, to fence, to apple;
   the call of a single goose flying toward
the north, for a moment emblematical
   in silhouette against the moonlit clouds;
and the flight of bats, swerving above the pasture—
   as if each moment bordered on disaster.

They orient themselves, in shuddering motion,
   by way of sounds they send out from themselves;
not too different, I suppose, from this attention
   I pay to my new surroundings—how my love's
propelled to seek its own reflection
   in outer forms, till what I see evolves
along more human lines—that is, toward story:
   we inhabit the habitat of allegory.

By this habit alone, perhaps, habitual
   voices out of sky and ditch are speaking you.
And something else today: a bell-like trill
   came through the hedge, through the window, drew

me toward a tufted titmouse, caught up in ritual
   tail-splay, wing-flex, lowered head, as if he knew
no more of the moment than this mating rage.
   I swear, somehow he made his eyes grow huge.

GOLDSMITH AND CHARITY

This modest print by Rembrandt
of a goldsmith finishing a statue
of a woman and two children
is nothing like the great portraits
that move me, move most of us, I think;
and yet it draws me in—by the way
the goldsmith's arm supports
the statue against his hip, exactly
as the woman in the statue holds
a child to her own; how
his other arm curves down
to the hammer in his hand, working
some obscure but necessary matter
of the sculpture's base; a motion matched
by her hand reaching down to stroke
the naked child who stands,
face in the folds of her robe.

The statue is a classical allegory,
a figure for the word *Charity,*
which in Rembrandt's engraving becomes
what I think of as a parable
of symmetry: the goldsmith
taking into his arms the statue
(just as she takes the children)
is the gesture of the artist
caring for that portion of the world
his art represents. And I see
how Rembrandt has taken care
to include the goldsmith's tools: forge
and anvil, apron, calipers and tongs, hatched
in the diligent repetitions of the needle's trace
on copper. The goldsmith's hands
are the calloused thick mitts of one
who has worked a lifetime in fire.

His eyes, lowered, seem closed
in dream, or prayer, fastened on
the hammerstroke—exactly where her eyes,
and the eyes of the held child, turn—
as though the artwork beheld the artisan
hammering from gold the word
whose alchemical ore is *dear*.

PARKED BENEATH A PEAR TREE

When I drove away,
the petals that had dropped
into the bed of my pickup
were picked up
in the wind curling
behind the cab. Lofted
in the wind-eddy, petals
whirling above sidepanels
fluttered in circles
but would not disperse,
so that for miles, all the way
to the clinic, I'm hauling
a small tornado.

I cannot say
why this drove me
to a flurry of joy,
any more than I have
wisdom to tell you
why a kind of brooding,
overcast weather has chosen
to settle over your body.
I can only listen, and attend,
and today, at least, offer
this telling—not much, if not
nothing: of small substance,
partial, slight, and blown.

NOVEMBER: JOURNAL ENTRY

The cat purrs us awake, pawing the pillow,
and our response, the day's first gesture,
is a gathering into each other's arms.
I remember this later, making the bed;
but she's not here, so I sit her stuffed bear
in her reading chair, open a book
of poems in its lap, her spare glasses
on its nose. Coming home, she'll know
I thought of her this way I can't express
—a small act that needed doing,
a moment that wanted, if not a monument,
then a makeshift, brown, fake-furred cairn.

When the dog whines in the backyard, I open up
my study window, and hoist him over the sill.
His squirming prompts a need in me to cry
"Incoming!" to warn the cat, before I drop
the blustery little dog-bomb on the rug.
This day of moments, of letting in the small
amusements, reminds me of something
long hidden under books and papers
on my desk; and so I knock off reading,
decide to take a drive. And what comes in,
but that other, familiar recognition—
of sorrow: an old man in a bus window, who,
through tinted glass, wears the face
of my father, so much so that I follow
beside it for blocks, backing up traffic, just
to hold myself a little longer near this man
who is not my father, but who is alive.

Slower now (that face moving on), I enter
a city park. On the pond's gray water
I see a single mallard. Next to the mallard,
easily a thousand or more Canada geese; and shimmering

among these, a dozen snow geese, and several pairs
of the tiny bufflehead, bobbing under like gophers;
also the elegant lines of hooded mergansers,
and shovelers, and green-winged teal, and one grebe,
rolling on its side to preen; and in the shallows
a great blue heron, tall and still, attentive
as a chaperone.
                    What words fly up
to meet these birds, this host? Abundance, yes,
and return—flocks and generations, focused by
the smallness of a city park, and here in spite of it.

All the mind has entertained today—
gestures between lovers, my foolish games,
these water birds—has come to settle in
the flat, gray space of my father's dying,
as if it were a pond: dog and doll
and duck, now the sun falling behind
that nameless goose-gray wash of cloud
that grows in the west this time of year at dusk.
The sun glows white like a nucleus inside.
The cloud's shallow edges fade to merest gauze—
not quite a formation, but something formed.

PINK SHEET

Yesterday late afternoon, on a pink flannel sheet on the grass,
        we lay under the sky, at the end
of your second summer; your first with focused eyes, and words:
        one for the soaring gray specks—*kite;*
one for the sudden straight bolt of brown—*dove;* but none yet
        for the silver satin sheen
of that sun-hemmed cloud; or the way the rain-wakened scent
        of soil beneath our sheet mingles
with blue, polished deep of sky; nor will there ever be
        a word for these, except *weather.*

"And there will always be weather." I tossed these words your way,
        knowing you can't catch them, but selfishly
hoping against them that you might remember
        this afternoon, when—flannel sheet—
we pointed out—potted impatiens—the numerous incarnations—
        cat's nose—of pink.

At dawn a prolonged windswell, the big pink business of clouds
        banking in on a cold front, bringing us now
this quiet expectancy. Glassy mist. Insects brought low,
        and waiting—the butterflies called "crescents"
are fanned out on the path, raising, lowering, testing their wings.
        And you're still closer to them
than to me—small enough you can approach, and touch;

        but when I so much as look
at the white patches in their wings, I freight them
        with memory: last night's moon,
as I patrolled the yard before bed, retrieving the stray
        toys and cups—a moon still and full,
silhouetting the low-scudding clouds, shivering the wisps
        of higher clouds, as if to taunt me
with distances. . . .

I know what lies beneath weather will go, too, one way or another—
        butterflies, a snail climbing a flowerpot,
things you admire frankly and without apparent need
        to commemorate them—will be gone
as your grandparents you never knew, as my father's parents
        I never knew, all this vast
forgetting: sliding under the moon, under weather,
        gathered up and folded
away, as easily as a pink sheet on a lawn.

INFANT FATHER

—Sophia

BIRTH

You entered screaming, anointed
with blood and vernix—
our tempestuous goddess,
weighed, cleaned, rubbed, recorded
by your priestess nurses.
When I held you in my hands,
I was the small one.

THREE A.M.

Still unfocused,
your pupils widen, glisten
beneath a nest
of Christmas lights I wove
around a lampshade above
the couch where we lie
in kindred amazement:
the lights you watch
the lights I watch you by.

THE FALL

Four months old, and this last hour
spent crying, crying hard.
Tears pool in a fold of your ear
like prayers that go unheard.

No sign of fever; you aren't cold.
No hunger to blame it on.
You're nursed, bathed, swaddled.
What else? —Original sin?

You're too young for ironies,
small Sophia, in my hands;
you cry, while I apologize
for what neither understands.

CLOSE

A father learns a certain way
to close a door. I grip
the knob as I would hold
a living thing,
and turn it slowly,
so that no errant click
of spindle, latch, or strikeplate
causes you to wake;
while my other hand
palms the door, to give
a guiding resistance:
striking that balance.

ROSES

You don't yet know we call them
        roses,
and it will be years before you understand
what I mean when I say that they've
        come back
from last year. No matter now:
        this morning
when I carry you toward them—
pink globes of sunlight in a breeze—
you smile, shriek, straighten your knees
        and lift,
in a kick, almost a leap, as if
        to spring
into flight. And I recall the phrase,
the babe leaped in the womb,
        but can't,
for a minute, remember where it's from;
and in that minute you,
        so recent
in the womb, and now in weather,
        seeing roses, leap
        again and again.

SERENADE

Had your mother not stirred
in bed and woken me,
I'd not have heard,
through the window, blackbirds
on the tin gray roofs
and chimney pots of Paris,
singing at dawn.

And in the journal
I kept from that trip,
I find this:
The offstage voice
in opera or play,
heard from the wings,
is token of all
that is at once
present and absent.

Coming and going—
we didn't know, that morning,
you were already
growing inside her.
Nor that I'd be hearing
blackbirds again, hearing
her sing to you,
from another room.

WORDS

Midwife crouched and urging,
nurse and nurse each supporting
legs of your mother: four women
doing the pure work of labor.
I attended with words that mattered
as little as noise from the hallway
to those four women. And then you.

When I held you, I kissed your brow,
and said the words I had rehearsed
for you, too new to know them—
mere ceremony
from the first man you'd meet.

Now as you ply your way
toward language, still far off,
we amuse ourselves, making sounds.
But I remember words
once spoken—and how, my dear,
we both must learn the burden
of words is making sounds cohere
with what abides in time.

CPSIA information can be obtained at www.ICGtesting.com
Printed in the USA
LVOW12s2142231014

410304LV00001B/249/P